Plays ...

GOD'S QUARTERBACK

HUDDLE UP, IT'S GAME TIME

Plays and Principles for the Pursuit of the Prize

GOD'S QUARTERBACK

HUDDLE UP, IT'S GAME TIME

ROSS E. WYCHE JR.

God's Quarterback: Huddle Up, It's Game Time

Plays and Principles for the Pursuit of the Prize

Ross E. Wyche Jr.

Published by RewNew Media
1st Edition
Printed in the U.S.A.

Cover design: Crystal Sinclair

Editor: Brian Moreland

ISBN: 978-0-578-78269-0

ACKNOWLEDGMENTS

I would first like to thank the Lord Jesus Christ for giving me the inspiration to write this book and share it with others. It has been a journey and He has been with me all of the way. Secondly, I would like to thank my best friend, chief editor and chief motivator—my wife Niya. If it wasn't for her, this book would still be incomplete. Thank you, honey.

I'd like to thank my children for wanting to read the book and asking, "Is it finished yet?" Thank you! I'd like to thank my mother for nurturing my passion for sports by taking me to all those practices and games as a youth.

Lastly, thank you to all of God's quarterbacks that paved the way for me and helped me along the way. Thank you for including me in your huddle.

CONTENTS

INTRODUCTION

The Preseason

Now you might be asking yourself what qualifies me to write a book about being God's quarterback? You're right in your thinking. I haven't led any team as a quarterback to a state title, national championship, or even far greater, the Super Bowl. I've never been on TV or graced the cover of *Sports Illustrated*. Nor have I ever made a news headline as a highly touted college recruit headed to a Power Five conference. So the questions loom: why then should you read this book? Why should you invest your precious time reading a book written by someone who wasn't drafted in the first round or played a successful career in the NFL? Why spend your hard-earned money listening to someone who doesn't have a rocket arm like Patrick Mahomes or run a 4.3 forty, a la Michael Vick, or for the new age, Lamar Jackson.

I will tell you why. When I was a little kid playing with friends in the backyard, sandlot, or schoolyard, I always wanted to be the quarterback. Didn't every kid who played football in the neighborhood want to be quarterback? I can remember nine times out of ten, if you brought the football, you were more than likely going to be the QB. You were the one who was going to draw up the plays in the dirt or on the football itself. You were the one who was going to evade the oncoming rusher as he yelled out, "One Mississippi, two Mississippi, three Mississippi...here I come," as you threw a dart past the second tree to little Johnny for a touchdown to lead your team to victory. As we got older the game switched from two-hand touch to tackle, and that's where you separated the boys from the men. Arguments and fights would ensue, but in the end, we would play again the next day.

The quarterback is a leader; the quarterback makes things happen; the quarterback has a lot riding on him; and in the game of life, it's no different. As men we are tasked with many things: being a leader in the workplace, being a leader in the home, and being a leader in our communities. So often men are being sacked under pressure, making the wrong decisions, or not making a decision at all, which ultimately leads them and the people they are leading to defeat.

You might be saying, "I'm not leading anyone. No one is following me. I'm not responsible for anyone." I would say that is simply not true. The most important person you are leading is yourself.

You might say, "Well, I'm not a good leader. I don't have that gift. I'm not a rah-rah guy." Here's what I say to that: "You *can* be a great leader. You *can* learn leadership and your personality is perfect."

You are exactly what God intended when He created you – remember that.

God can and wants to use you to do great things with the talent He's given you. He has given you authority and dominion to lead others to victory. God has chosen you to be his quarterback. In essence, you are God's quarterback! So what qualifies me to write this book? That's easy. My deep understanding of football as a lifelong fan combined with my education in seminary and my passion for doing God's work in the game of life. God has called upon me to be His quarterback and spread His message, and I have accepted. During the course of this book, using the metaphor of playing football, my objective is to teach you plays and principles that will help you become God's quarterback and discover your true purpose.

1ST QUARTER

"

As God's quarterback you must know God's word. Study to show thyself approved.

CHAPTER 1

The Pardon

While I was growing up in Massachusetts during the 1980s, the New England Patriots weren't even remotely close to the dynasty-slash-juggernaut they were from 2001-2019, led by arguably the greatest quarterback of all time: Tom Brady. The Patriots of the '80s were decent; matter of fact, in 1986 they reached the Super Bowl to face the very talented Chicago Bears that included quarterback Jim McMahon, Hall-of-Fame running back Walter Payton, and William "The Refrigerator" Perry. New England suffered a bludgeoning loss as they were defeated 46-10. Before they drafted Drew Bledsoe, and before Tony Eason assumed the quarterback position, New England experimented with an undersized but uniquely talented quarterback by the name of Doug Flutie.

A native of Massachusetts, Doug Flutie played his high school football in the town of Natick, and upon graduating from Natick high school, he took his talents to Boston

College. It was at Boston College where he went on to win the Heisman Trophy, an award given to the best player in college football, and where he is infamously known for the last-second "Hail Flutie" pass that beat the Miami Hurricanes in November 1984. I can remember seeing that highlight repeatedly as a little boy. Doug Flutie was and still is a legend, but the thing you may not know about Flutie was that he was considered too short for a quarterback. Doug Flutie is listed at a lengthy five feet, nine inches. Most NFL scouts and coaches consider any quarterback under six feet to be a risk. However, the Patriots gave Flutie a chance (after he went to the Canadian Football League first, shout out to Canada!) because they knew the size of his heart was off the charts.

During the 2019 NFL draft, there was another quarterback whose height was in question. He listed at five feet, ten inches and one eighth. He too, like Doug Flutie, won the Heisman Trophy, once again being recognized as college football's best player. His name is Kyler Murray, who played for Oklahoma. Why am I bringing these two individuals up and why am I emphasizing their height? I'm glad you asked. Whereas NFL scouts will scrutinize a person's size and stature in regards to playing quarterback, God does not. NFL scouts and coaches will discriminate due to a person's makeup but God will not. God is concerned about the individual's inner makings. He is concerned about your heart. God historically throughout the

Bible used people who were considered unpopular choices. David was a boy who slayed Goliath. Paul was out to destroy the church but became the greatest evangelist there was. And Peter denied Jesus three times but then went on to become one of the greatest disciples in history.

I want you to know that if you want to play on God's team, if you want to play quarterback for God, if you want to carry out His plan and win for Him, then be not dismayed. God does not look at your size, your background, or your shortcomings. God accepts you as you are and accepts you where you are. He does not discriminate. He doesn't care if you are five feet, nine inches or six feet nine. He wants you, and if you want Him, then you can play on God's team. He wants you, my brother, to be His quarterback. Are you ready to be God's quarterback?

The first thing you must do is join God's team. This will be the most important thing that you will ever do you in your life. And get this, it doesn't take long to do. You don't have to train at the gym or practice running the 40-yard dash as those who are preparing for the draft. You don't have to hire an agent or tryout for God's team. There's no interview, no background check, no experience needed.

So what does it take to join God's team?

Before I answer that question, I remember growing up being the biggest Dallas Cowboys fan; and this was before the 1990s when they won three Super Bowls with Troy Aikman, Emmitt Smith, and Michael Irvin. The Cowboys I'm referring to were the Cowboys of the 1980s with the likes of Danny White, Tony Dorsett, and Drew Pearson and they became known as "America's Team." Well, let me tell you, being on God's team is far greater and more important than being on America's team. By being on God's team you will be equipped to do great things for the kingdom, much more than winning a Super Bowl. You will be able to win souls for Jesus Christ. Your life will be more fulfilling than you can possibly imagine, because you will be living for a higher purpose. And God rewards those who play for His team.

So how do you join God's Team?

It's not hard but the first thing you must understand is *why* must you join God's team. The story starts a long time ago when the first man and woman that God created, Adam and Eve, were in the Garden of Eden. God gave them dominion over the earth and the charge to live responsibly in the land that He created. God is a loving father; in fact,

God is love, but one thing He desires from His children is obedience. He gives us the ability to choose between right and wrong. In other words, God gives us free will. But He desires that we obey Him and do what is right. He gives us quarterbacks the opportunity to change the play at the line of scrimmage, but we must live with the results if our choice deviates from His plan.

God gave Adam and Eve a lot of freedom to do what they wanted, yet the one thing God prohibited them to do they did. Adam and Eve failed miserably. I mean, this was an epic fail that affected mankind long after. Remember when you were a kid and you did something you weren't supposed to do? You knew that when your mom or dad found out, they were not going to be happy. You knew you would be in big, big trouble, but you did it anyway. This is what happened with Adam and Eve. God told them, "You are free to eat from any tree in the garden, but you must *not* eat from the Tree of Knowledge, of good and evil, for when you eat from it, you will certainly die." So what did they go and do? Despite being given that very clear rule, Adam and Eve disobeyed God and ate fruit from the forbidden Tree.

Adam and Eve fumbled in a major way, but they had some help in coughing this one up. A talking serpent known as Satan approached Eve. Satan is one of the craftiest individuals around and his whole aim is to wreak havoc in your life. Satan is on the opposing team and he is out to steal, kill, and ultimately defeat those who are not on his team. I want to make something clear:

If you are not on God's team, then you are on the opposing team.

If you are not on God's team, then you are lost.

And Satan loves to recruit those who are lost.

Now getting back to the story: Satan approached Eve and questioned her, "Did God really say you must not eat from any tree in the garden? You will certainly not die. For God knows that when you eat from it your eyes will be opened, and you will be like God, knowing good and evil."

Remember, Satan is crafty. He can dial up defenses that will confuse some of God's greatest quarterbacks. Satan can disguise different looks, order up different blitz packages, and he can keep you guessing. He is an offensive coordinator's nightmare. Why? Because Satan is relentless and doesn't play by the rules. He operates by any means necessary. Don't sleep on Satan. Don't be scared but don't sleep.

Now I want to back up a little, because you may be asking, "Well, what happened to Adam and Eve?" You might also be saying, "You still haven't told me how to join God's team." Lastly, you might be wondering, "Now, why do I want to join God's team again?"

As a result of Adam and Eve eating from the Tree of Knowledge, the world in which they lived would be changed forever. Their eyes were opened and they realized they were naked. Adam and Eve's disobedience created what became known as the "Original Sin" or the first sin. Let me explain what sin is in layman's terms.

> **Sin is an act against God, something He would not approve of.**

Adam and Eve's first sin caused separation from God. They hid from God in the garden because they knew what they had done was wrong. Adam and Eve were naked and afraid. They were convicted by their own actions, so they hid. Let me tell you something: there is nowhere you can go that God cannot find you. God is omnipresent (He's everywhere).

Because of their lack of obedience, Adam and Eve were kicked out of the Garden of Eden and cursed. They would be subjected to great pain and intense labor of the land. More importantly, they would not escape death. Sin separated them from God and ultimately they lost the ability to live forever. Death, my friends, is the result of their sin.

So why join God's team?

Well, as another result of Adam and Eve's sin, all humans who are birthed into this world will start out disconnected from God. But there is One who can reconnect you. Jesus Christ is the only one who can reconnect you to the loving Father. When you are reconnected to God, death is still unavoidable, but you will live again in the heavenly realm with God, your Heavenly Father. I must add that in order for that to happen, God had to give up something very near and dear to Himself. God sacrificed his only begotten son, Jesus Christ, in order to save the world from their sins.

God sacrificed His son for *you*.

Why? Because God loves *you* that much.

When you join God's team, you are able to have a relationship with the Father and enjoy the fellowship of the Father. It is important to always remember: this fellowship came with a price. God desires that all people on earth would come to know Him through His son, Jesus Christ.

God doesn't care about how many mistakes you've made. He will accept you as you are. The question is, will you accept and receive Him as your Lord and Savior?

Since I'm a sports junkie, let me put it in the football vernacular. God doesn't care about how many interceptions you've thrown, how many fumbles you've lost, or if you forgot the snap count. God loves you despite your mishaps and He doesn't hang them over your head and constantly remind you how you came up short on fourth and one. God doesn't keep count of all your mistakes and replay them over and over again on the ten-o'clock news. You won't be featured on the blooper real or be made fun of. Because guess what, we all fall short because none of us are perfect. God is the only true and perfect being in existence.

So you may be asking, "How do I join God's team? How do I join the greatest team ever assembled? How do I sign up and when can I start?"

If you are ready for your life to change, if you are ready to be God's quarterback, then let's do it. The Bible says in **Romans 10:9**: "If you confess with your mouth, 'Jesus is Lord,' and believe in your heart that God raised Him from the dead, you will be saved."

If you are ready, pray this prayer:

Dear Jesus, I am a sinner and I need your forgiveness. I believe that you died for my sins and rose from the dead to defeat death once and for all. Because of my faith in you, I now have eternal life and a relationship with my Heavenly Father. Jesus, teach me now how to live for you. In Jesus name I pray. Amen.

I'm extremely excited for you and I welcome you onto God's team. You are now ready to be God's quarterback... let's get started with God's playbook.

CHAPTER 2

The Playbook

Now that you have finished celebrating your new life in Christ, it's time to get to work. Similar to being drafted in the NFL, whether it be in the 1st round or 7th round, the most important fact remains: you've been called by God onto His team (you've been drafted). Unlike the NFL, even though you've been drafted to this team, you can never be cut, put on waivers, placed on a practice squad, or traded to a different team, for that matter. You will always be a member of God's team. You will always be God's quarterback. The apostle Paul tells us in **Romans 8:38-39**, "For I am sure that neither death nor life, nor angels nor rulers, nor things present nor things to come, nor powers, nor height nor depth, nor anything else in all creation, will be able to separate us from the love of God in Christ Jesus our Lord."

I want you to know there is nothing that you or anyone else could do that could separate you from God's love or

His team. You might be thinking, "Ross, you don't know my checkered past."

I'm here to tell you, "Nothing!"

You might say, "But I just did something bad, beyond forgiveness, beyond repair!"

Read my lips, "Nothing."

Now let me explain something. You may have done wrong and committed a sin and still be a part of God's team (a full recipient of His love), but there will be consequences for your actions. I can recall when I was a young boy I did something mischievous; I got in trouble for playing with fire. I had found my mother's lighter and an old pack of cigarettes. I decided I was going to try and do what the adults did. I went out back and tried to light a cigarette, but in the process of lighting it I burned my hand. I was in a great deal of pain. I remember calling my mother at work and telling her that I had burned my hand while cooking hot dogs in the microwave. As you could probably guess, Mom saw right through that one and I finally confessed. Now here is the point I'm trying to make: I was punished for trying to smoke and for lying. My mom was upset with me and she let me have it, but never once did she stop loving me. Never once did my action jeopardize my status of being her child. I would always be her son and nothing could deter that. In the same fashion, we can and we will make mistakes (sin), but nothing can separate us from God's love and from being a part of His family. I wish more people understood that. It's in God's playbook, the Bible, written in His word.

I mentioned that I grew up watching the New England Patriots as a kid and even now as an adult. We discussed Doug Flutie and the height challenges he overcame to be quarterback in the NFL. Well, there was another New England quarterback who faced some challenges on draft day, and his name is Tom Brady. You see, before Tom Brady won six Super Bowls with the Patriots and became known as "Tom Terrific" (a name which he despises, therefore we will no longer use that nickname), he was a 6th round draft pick out of the University of Michigan, selected 199th out of 254. Because of being picked late in the draft, Tom Brady always played with a chip on his shoulder. And Tom Brady went on to be arguably the greatest quarterback of all time. So, what am I trying to say? It doesn't matter *when* you join God's team. The most important thing is joining God's team and making the most of your opportunity when you do. Remember, joining God's team as God's quarterback is a privilege and an honor. Remember, Christ died for you.

After understanding your place on God's team as God's quarterback, you have to understand what His plan is for the team and how that plan will ultimately lead you and those you lead to Godly success. It's time to get into God's playbook: the Bible. The one thing that makes a great quarterback is that he understands the playbook. He's in concert with what the coach wants him to accomplish. The

QB knows the concept and scheme the coach is trying to convey. A good quarterback is an extension of the coach; in essence, the quarterback is the coach on the field. When you are in God's word, or what I call the "playbook," you know what God wants you to do. You know the play. You know where God wants you to line up. When God calls a play, you better believe it's the right play to execute.

Now, here's the funny thing: sometimes God will call a play that doesn't make sense to you; but guess what, you need to run the play anyway. He knows best. Remember, He's God and you are not. He's all knowing and omniscient. There have been times in my life where God has called a play that seemed bizarre to me. He's called plays that I didn't think I could carry out, but His plays are always well-designed and when executed properly, they are unstoppable. Some plays are simple and some are complex, but at the end of the day, God calls them because He believes you can execute them.

Some of the best coach/quarterback relationships in NFL history have worked because there was a great trust between the coach/quarterback. In New England, Tom Brady and Bill Belichick had a great relationship because there was a great trust and mutual respect they had for one another. Bill Walsh and Joe Montana had a great relationship. Peyton Manning and Tony Dungy, Jim Kelly and Marv Levy, etc. The list goes on and on but you get my point. You might have some other quarterback and coach pairings you might want to highlight; I know I missed a few.

It is important for the quarterback to know the playbook because, frankly, when the game is on the line he must know what to do in the heat of the moment. If a quarterback does not know the plays, there is no way he can effectively play the game. He will be lost, and more importantly, those playing alongside him will lose. If the QB is a husband, his wife is in harm's way. If he is a father, his children are in jeopardy. If he is a leader in the workplace, his team can be in the crosshairs of defeat.

The apostle Paul wrote the epistle (letter) "2Timothy" to his young protégé. In **2 Timothy 2:15**, Paul said, "Study to show thyself approved." In other words, he was telling Timothy to present himself as one approved by God to correctly handle the word of God. Timothy had the responsibility to understand God's word, to be on guard against those who may misuse God's word or misconstrue His word. We have to know God's word for ourselves.

**As God's quarterback
you must know God's word.**

God's quarterback must study to show thyself approved. We must get in our playbook (God's word, the Bible) and study. We must meditate on His word. Even as I write this book, it is requiring me to get into His word as to not misquote or misdirect those who are reading it.

You might be asking yourself, "How often do I need to open up my playbook and for how long do I need to read God's playbook? Do I need to read the playbook aloud or silently? In the morning or at night?" As God's quarterback, these are very good questions, and frankly there is no right answer. I do have some questions for you though:

What type of quarterback are you trying to be?

Are you trying to be a backup QB that doesn't play much but should be ready at all times?

Are you trying to be a starting quarterback that plays but doesn't play well because they aren't maximizing their potential?

Lastly, are you trying to be an All-Pro, or better yet, are you striving to be a Hall of Famer? If you answered that you are striving to be a Hall of Famer, I would encourage you to get into your playbook as much as possible. There is so much to learn in God's playbook; the Bible never gets old and there is always a nugget you can find and apply to your life. There have been times in my life where I have read a passage of scripture several times and then come back to it years later and find something that I never saw before from the same passage. God is good.

As I mentioned before, it is important to learn the playbook and keep studying the playbook. The one thing that has made Tom Brady such a great quarterback is his attention to detail. He knows his playbook. He is always trying to gain an edge, always trying to improve, on the field and in life. If you watch him during the game, while seated at the bench he is looking at the defense's formation on the tablet trying to see how he can defeat the enemy and win the game.

Your job is to know your playbook so you can lead your team to victory. Remember, knowledge is power, the more you know the better you can perform.

So I ask you today, what kind of quarterback do you want to be for God?

Get to reading His playbook (the word of God).

2ND QUARTER

"

Jesus Christ will strenghten you and through Him you can do it. Not through your strength but through His strength.

CHAPTER 3

The Position

The quarterback position is the most talked about position in football but also arguably the most important position. There are highly paid individuals who are tasked with scouting, interviewing, and testing quarterbacks to see which one will hopefully lead their team to the "Promised Land" (Super Bowl Champions). These individuals go through great lengths year after year to make sure they have found the right quarterback. Sometimes they pick the right one and sometimes they fail. When they fail their quarterback is considered a "bust." My goal is to make sure you are not labeled a "bust."

There is nothing worse than wasted talent. There's nothing worse than being labeled as "someone who has potential." Potential doesn't get you anywhere unless you do something with it. There have been a great deal of quarterbacks who had potential but due to their off field problems, lack of work ethic, or inability to execute, they are no longer in the league. Life in the NFL is short and life in general is short. I urge you to avoid wasting your talent. Instead:

Use your talent to serve as God's quarterback.

The quarterback is the position everyone wants to play growing up but the question is why, why does everyone want to play quarterback? Personally, I think it is because they always have the football in their hands. You can have complete control of your team's offense and influence scoring touchdowns. You make decisions that can alter the course of the game. You decide where to go with the ball. Are you throwing deep or out into the flat? Are you tucking the ball and taking off for the end zone? When it boils down to it, the quarterback is a position of power. However, as the old saying goes, with power comes great responsibility. If you are still reading this book, one thing you must understand: you are called to be God's quarterback and with that calling comes great responsibility. There's an endless amount of people counting on you. Huddle up!

Every kid wants to be quarterback but for my novice football fans (my wife included), we need to understand what the quarterback actually does and what he is responsible for. Football is a great game but I admit it can be difficult to understand. In the same vein, God's word is amazing but at times it can be difficult to understand as well. Hang in there. The more you read and study the scriptures, the more God's word will make sense, like football.

Back to the quarterback position. So much goes into the QB position other than being the face of the franchise and signing lucrative multi-million-dollar contracts and doing yogurt commercials (sorry Dak Prescott). Quick sidebar, as I mentioned earlier, I am a Dallas Cowboys fan. For those who are not, please don't hold it against me (please keep reading this book). As it so happens, I'm in the airport now, headed to Philadelphia with a Dallas Cowboys shirt on. Philadelphia Eagles' fans can be a little rowdy, or should I say *passionate*, when it comes to our teams' rivalry. Please pray for me.

Let us start first with the quarterback's first responsibility on the field: they receive the play. In other words, the quarterback knows the play to be executed before anyone else in the offensive huddle does. The quarterback receives the play from the coach who has designed the play, which came from the playbook. These days, the coach relays the play from his headset to the speakers inside the quarterback's helmet. A great quarterback understands that the key to success and staying on the football field stems from listening to his coach and doing what his coach asks him to do. As God's quarterback, we must listen to our coach

(God) and do what He says. Scripture tells us about listening to God and doing what He says in **James 1:22**: "But be doers of the word, and not hearers only." There have been many a quarterback who heard what the coach said but decided to do their own thing. We must embrace the fact that God knows better than we do. He created us. He created this world and He knows everything that has happened and will happen. When God gives you a play from his playbook, listen to Him and do what He says.

Once the quarterback receives the play from his coach, he is responsible for relaying that play to the team in the huddle. All the offensive players have a certain responsibility that they must carry out as it pertains to the play. As God's quarterback, you and I are responsible for receiving God's play from Him and relaying it to those who we come into contact with: family, friends, and our community. Here's the thing: if we don't receive God's word, we can't help those we are leading (our teammates). We have to make sure we are receiving God's word.

The question is, how do you receive God's play?

> **God's play is received by reading His word. God's word reveals who He is and what His plan is.**

How does God speak to God's quarterback? He speaks through His word. In the beginning of the Gospel according to John, he says, "In the beginning was the Word, and the Word was with God, and the Word was God." My fellow quarterbacks, the Word of God is God, therefore do what it says. Don't be a renegade. Renegade quarterbacks throw interceptions, fumble the ball, and get sacked. By disregarding their coach's play and trying to do things their way, renegade quarterbacks can hurt their team, and ultimately lose the game. In football, the costs of losing are living with defeat and the feeling that you've let down your team. In real life, the losses can be even more impactful when you ignore God's play calls and let down your family, friends, or those who rely on you to lead them.

Once the quarterback has shared the play with the other players in the huddle, the team lines up on the line of scrimmage. It is the quarterback's job to make sure everyone is lined up in the right spot. He's making sure the linemen have the right protection called and the running backs have the right depth. As he surveys the field, the quarterback might have the wide receiver go in motion to see if the defense is playing man coverage or zone coverage. In addition to that, he needs to make sure if the tight end needs to be in the slot or off the line of scrimmage or covered.

If you have never watched a football game, your head might be spinning right now. But if you watch football like

I do, this is some fascinating stuff. Once everyone on the offense is set, the quarterback will tell the center when to hike the football (start the play). The quarterback determines when the play will start. Might I add that the quarterback has 40 seconds from the end of the previous play to do all the things I just mentioned? He has to be efficient with his time because if he takes longer than the 40 seconds, the team will be penalized for "Delay of Game." As God's quarterback you need to make sure you are fulfilling God's play in a timely fashion, because if you don't, others around you may suffer from your delay. Remember again:

> **It's one thing to hear from God; it's another thing to put into action what He has told you to do.**

God's quarterback has a lot on his plate: hear the play from the coach, call the play in the huddle or at the line, then finally, after the center snaps the ball, the quarterback has to execute the play. Let's talk about execution. In some instances, the execution might be as simple as handing the ball off to your running back and then getting out of the way. Other plays may call for a RPO (Run/Pass Option) or throw to an open receiver and just let the ball rip downfield. Executing a simple play can have its challenges. For instance, are you playing on the road or at home? Sometimes it is hard to block out the noise. Are you playing in sunny Miami or in the Frozen Tundra, otherwise known as Lambeau Field in Green Bay, Wisconsin? Conditions are rarely perfect but the game must go on. It is the same in life. When God calls upon you to do something of significance, there is always something else happening. Life doesn't stop; it's constant and comes with many challenges. The question is, when God calls upon you, will you execute or not? No excuses. You must execute. And I believe you will.

When it comes to execution, one of the best quarterbacks to ever do it was Joe Montana, a 4-time Super Bowl champion with the San Francisco 49ers. His nickname was "Cool Joe" because he was cool under pressure. When circumstances were at their most difficult, Cool Joe would perform at the highest level. Being a Dallas fan who watched the 49ers beat the Cowboys in the playoffs during Montana's reign, for me to utter the name Joe Montana can almost be viewed as sacrilegious; but Montana was that good. His legend started at the University of Notre Dame where he led the Fighting Irish to a come-from-behind win in the 1979 Cotton Bowl against the University of Houston Cougars. Leading your team from behind is one thing, but being able to execute at a high level in frigid temperatures is another. It gets even better though; in the midst of icy weather, Montana was also dealing with the flu and a high-grade fever. Despite those challenges and being behind in the 4th quarter, Cool Joe Montana found the inner strength to lead his team to victory. *That* is executing at a high level. When the pressure is on, can you execute God's plan for your life? The answer is an emphatic *yes*! Remember, scripture tell us in **Philippians 4:13**: "I can do all things through Christ [Jesus] who strengthens me." Remember that verse when you are dealing with a hard situation that seems impossible to handle or get through.

> **Jesus Christ will strengthen you and through Him you can do it. Not through your strength but through His strength.**

When you (God's quarterback) have the confidence that God can help you through anything, your teammates' confidence will be strengthened as well.

One more story about "Cool Joe" that I think you will appreciate. This story is about as legendary as they come. It's a story that points out Montana's ability to execute and lead at the highest level and on the greatest stage. It was Super Bowl XXIII (23 for those not fluent in Roman numerals) in late January 1989. The San Francisco 49ers were playing the Cincinnati Bengals and trailing by 3 points in the 4th quarter with roughly 3 minutes left in the game. The 49ers had the ball on the 8-yard line, 92 yards away from victory. The challenge is set before the 49ers' offense, and Joe Montana enters the huddle. The pressure is intense. Fans are holding their breath. It's go time. Joe buttons his chinstrap and looks down the field in the direction they need to go and calmly says, "Oh, look there's John Candy at the back of the end zone in the stands." Talk about being cool under pressure. Joe Montana wasn't aloof or irresponsible. This was Joe's way of indirectly saying, "Hey, we are going to get this done, relax. No sense being uptight. Let's go out and perform." Joe Montana had ice water in his veins. As God's quarterback, you need to be a calming presence as you lead your team to victory. The people you lead are watching you and taking cues from you. Will you wilt or will you lead with confidence and win. On that legendary drive, Cool Joe led his offense 92 yards to the end zone, and his team to becoming the Super Bowl champions.

CHAPTER 4

The Pass Rush

I think it is important for us to understand something before we go any further. In the world of football just like there are scouts, front office executives, coaches, and owners looking to find that perfect quarterback to lead their franchise to the Super Bowl, these same individuals are looking for players to counter that quarterback on the defensive side of the ball. Then there's the opposing fans rooting for the other team. Not everybody loves and roots for the quarterback or God's quarterback. As I mentioned before, since the beginning of time Satan's main responsibility has been to wreak havoc on God's children. Satan has always wanted and still wants to disrupt the plans God has for His children. Satan wants to be the main focus. He wants power but for all the wrong reasons.

Let's examine Satan's fall. Satan's fall was due mainly to pride. He wanted to be God and there was only one God. Satan had a good gig; he was one of God's angels but that wasn't good enough. Satan's desire to be God caused our Heavenly Father to remove him from heaven.

As you can imagine, Satan is not happy about being kicked out of heaven and he's not happy with God, therefore Satan has sights on rushing the passer. Who is the passer? The passer is you, God's quarterback. Satan is up day and night disguising the ultimate signature move known as "The Pass Rush." He is trying to get past your offensive line and create pressure off the edge, up the middle, or from the slot. If he can get to you and apply pressure, Satan's hope is that he can cause you or I to make a mistake: an errant throw, take a sack, or ultimately put the ball on the ground (fumble).

In everyday life, we will be faced with different challenges and circumstances that might surprise us, but we must remember that "The Pass Rush" from an opposing defense is part of the game. I will share later in the chapter how we can handle the pass rush; first I want to tell you about some of the best pass rushers to ever play the game and what made them so effective.

One of the greatest pass rushers of all time was Lawrence Taylor of the New York Giants. He had it all—size, power, and speed. He would come off the edge and just give the opposing team's left tackle fits. Coaches playing against Lawrence Taylor would have to game-plan against him. The coaches' main focus was how are we going to block this guy. When the offense broke from the huddle, everyone was searching for L.T. They had to know where he was lined up. Not only was Lawrence Taylor physically imposing, he was also a mean, nasty guy on the field. He liked to trash talk. He tried to intimidate his opponents and psych them out. He wanted to let the quarterback know that he was coming and with reckless abandon.

In college while playing for the North Carolina Tar Heels, Lawrence Taylor was a unanimous All-American and also was selected as the ACC Player of the Year. He went on to have an illustrious career, playing 13 seasons with the New York Giants. He was a two-time Super Bowl champion, ten-time Pro Bowler, and named the Most Valuable Player in 1986. In spite of all those accolades, Lawrence Taylor will mostly be remembered for one of the most gruesome injuries in football history.

On November 18, 1985, in Washington, DC, the Giants were playing their conference rivals, the Washington Redskins. Taylor, as he normally did, was wreaking havoc that night, and on this particular play, he rushed the passer and sacked Joe Theismann, and in the process broke his leg. It was an extremely bad break, a compound fracture. Unfortunately, Joe Theismann never played another down of football again.

After the incident happened, Lawrence Taylor shared that he never meant to hurt Joe or ruin his career. But the same can't be said for Satan. You see, Satan is intentionally trying to end your career. He wants to knock you out of the game. He wants to cause you pain. He wants to sack you. And if he gives you a gruesome injury, Satan has zero remorse.

They say "defense" wins games and there have been some great defenders and great defenses throughout history. Some defenders and some defenses can often take over a game and dominate the opposing team, giving quarterbacks fits. When I was growing up, I remember the New England Patriots reached the Super Bowl to play the infamous Chicago Bears. The Bears had a good team but they had an even greater defense. The Bears played the "46 Defense," which applied nonstop pressure, showing different blitz packages. The leader of that group was an undersized ferocious linebacker by the name of Mike Singletary. The Singletary-led defense applied all kinds of pressure on New England's quarterbacks, Tony Eason and Steve Grogan, and defeated the Patriots 46-10 that day.

The Baltimore Ravens had another great defense led by another great leader by the name of Ray Lewis. During his career, Ray Lewis led the Ravens to two Super Bowl victories. He neutralized offenses with his speed and tenacity. He studied his opponents by watching film. He studied their tendencies. He memorized their schemes, and in some instances, he knew what the offense was going to do simply by the way they lined up after breaking the huddle. I can say without hesitation that Ray Lewis studied to "show thyself approved."

The last two guys I mentioned, Mike Singletary and Ray Lewis, were speed guys. They played fast and downhill with their ears pinned back. They played with reckless abandon, but the next couple of men I want to highlight were the opposite; they were big guys with brute strength. These men were predominantly double-teamed. One man couldn't block these guys. Sometimes it required two linemen, sometimes a lineman and a tight end. In some cases, offenses would use a lineman and then chip these pass rushers with a running back. Michael Strahan of the New York Giants is one of the all-time sacks leaders who has now made a nice career in television. Back in his pro-football days, Strahan utilized his power with incredible leverage and a motor that wouldn't stop. He was a man on a mission that wouldn't stop until he reached the quarterback, and once he did, the quarterback was on the ground.

The late great Reggie White, known as the "Minister of Defense," played for the Green Bay Packers. He too was a Super Bowl champion and was the former all-time sack leader during his playing career. At times, it seemed as if Reggie White had superhuman strength when he was on the field. He seemed like a man among boys. Reggie had a patented move where he would get up under an offensive lineman—a 300-plus-pound lineman—and then commence to throw him in the air. It was such an act of strength but Reggie White made it look effortless.

Now you may be wondering why I am talking about

defense and spending so much time describing how elite defensive players played the game. You might be thinking, "I thought this book was about quarterbacks." You are correct but I want to show you that although defense wins games in football, any defense can be defeated by an equipped and well-prepared offense. The name of the game is *preparation* and knowing what your defense is doing. Using the tools in your tool chest will help you be victorious in battle.

Some of the best quarterbacks to ever play the game were also some of the greatest students of the game. If you are going to step onto the field as a quarterback, there are some things that you must know. First of all, you must know your opponent. You need to know their moves and their tendencies. In other words, you must *study* your opponent. As God's quarterback, you have to be aware of the tricks and snares the enemy is attempting to trip you up with.

You have to be ready for the spiritual warfare that comes with being God's quarterback. The Bible says in **1 Peter 5:8**: "Be sober-minded; be watchful. Your adversary the devil prowls around like a roaring lion, seeking someone to devour." The enemy is not your friend.

James 4:7 says: "Submit yourselves therefore to God. Resist the devil, and he will flee from you." Satan will try and disguise his approach and try to come across as your friend, but understand there's nothing friendly about what he's trying to accomplish. Study your opponent and be alert. His pass rush is ferocious. For even Satan disguises himself as the angel of light.

I liken being alert to having great *pocket presence.* What is pocket presence? Good question, let's first define a *pocket.* A pocket is the area behind the offensive line that a quarterback uses to set his feet and make a throw to his receivers. If you have a clean pocket the quarterback has the ability to step into his throw and make an accurate pass. Sometimes the pocket can be crowded with defenders that make it difficult for a quarterback to make a good throw. Defenders are coming from all angles. Most of the time, the quarterback can't see where they are coming from, so he must anticipate and slide to his left or right, step up in the pocket, or escape the pocket when it is overtaken by the pass rushers. Having pocket presence is the ability to feel or know when it's time to move, almost an innate ability.

As God's quarterback, I talked about being on alert and not being distracted. When a quarterback has great pocket presence, he knows he must keep his eyes downfield even in the midst of a pass rush. The quarterback can't get "happy feet" in the pocket; he must stand in the pocket and trust his protection from his linemen. Sometimes you have to "Be still and know that I am God…" (**Psalm 46:10**).

You have to know when to stay still and when to move—that's having pocket presence. Now don't misunderstand me. Sometimes you are going to get hit; that's part of being a quarterback—and especially God's quarterback—but you have to understand if God be for me, who can be against me? That's knowing who your opponent is and always being aware of their pass rush to stop you.

3RD QUARTER

"

As God's quarterback you have to care about God's people, or more profoundly, you have to <u>love</u> God's people.

CHAPTER 5

The Power Formation

There are two pro football teams I root for in my house: the Dallas Cowboys and Baltimore Ravens. Before we moved to Dallas in 2004, we lived in Baltimore and I was a Ravens fan. I remember them winning their first Super Bowl, and at the time, I was working for a staffing company named Aerotek (owned by Steve Bisciotti, the team's owner). Steve purchased the Ravens from Art Modell that year, and they went on to win the Super Bowl that same year. I think it is fair to say that the Baltimore Ravens were a great investment for Steve Bisciotti. Fast forward to 2019, the Ravens were on their way to making some noise during the playoff season on a quest for their third Super Bowl in team history. They were doing it riding the coattails of their MVP quarterback, Lamar Jackson. Alas, they only made it to the second round of playoffs that year, getting knocked out by the Tennessee Titans. But the Ravens still had an impressive season.

Lamar Jackson is an exceptional quarterback and I think that is an understatement. He is a rare talent because he can beat you with his arm and with his legs. He can beat you inside the pocket or outside the pocket. In 2019, he broke the single-season rushing record for a quarterback, recently held by Michael Vick, with two games still left to be played. Lamar has continued to prove the naysayers wrong with his play week in and week out. It goes without saying that he truly is a generational talent; no one has ever seen a quarterback like Lamar Jackson. People will try and compare him to others, but quite frankly, there is no other comparison. He's fast, elusive, and he's a winner. He will do whatever it takes to win the game.

As I reflect on Lamar Jackson's football talent and skill, I would be remiss not to comment on his most impressive characteristic above all. As stated before, Lamar Jackson is a gifted quarterback (notice I didn't say "athlete" because he's a quarterback first, then an athlete); but he's an extremely humble young man. You won't hear Lamar Jackson talking about himself or focusing on his own individual statistics. You will, however, hear him talking about his teammates and his coaching staff. He knows that there is no "I" in "team." The Bible says, "Humble yourselves before the Lord, and he will exalt you." As God's quarterback, we don't have to elevate ourselves or toot our own horn; let the Lord do that. Stay humble and watch the Lord work.

I believe the Ravens did a terrific job of putting Lamar

Jackson in an environment where he could use his gifts and talents. The coaches crafted their offense around his God-given abilities. They took a page out of the playbooks of old and played power football. They used formations that aligned with their personnel. The Baltimore Ravens, for the most part, lined up every down in a "Power Formation." They used fullbacks and multiple tight ends and created mismatches against opposing defenses. They enforced their will against their opponents with Lamar Jackson at the helm. The Ravens' offense took the NFL by storm and man was it exciting to watch.

For you and I as God's quarterbacks, we are most successful when we put ourselves in the Power Formation. The Power Formation for us as believers is having a relationship with God through His Son, Jesus Christ. It is also walking in and with the Holy Spirit.

The Holy Trinity is the Power Formation.

The Holy Trinity Power Formation is impossible to stop. When we walk in the Spirit as God's quarterback, we can be confident that we will overcome all obstacles that come our way. The enemy can throw different looks at us but he will fail to stop what God has put in motion. For the Bible says, "Being confident of this, that He who began a good work in you will carry it on to completion until the day of Christ Jesus" (**Philippians 1:6**). You have to believe and keep the faith. I know that through the process of writing this book—and it's been a long process—I have encountered obstacles: work, car trouble, busyness, procrastination, etc. You know, sometimes we are our own worst enemy. But if you take a step back and realign yourself with the Father, Son, and the Holy Spirit, then you will get back on track. Just believe.

In 2004, I was on the way back from a business conference in Texas. I had just visited with my father-in-law, and he asked what my plans were and what I wanted to do. I proceeded to tell him that I was throwing around the notion of going to seminary full time but didn't quite know where yet. We talked about other things that night and then I went on my way. Well, later that week on the shuttle back to DFW airport, the Holy Spirit told me that we were coming to Dallas. So upon my landing back in Maryland, I told my wife we are moving to Texas and that we did. The Holy Spirit led us to Texas, and I say the Lord "led us" there, because it was very clear.

Now why am I telling you about the Holy Spirit telling me what to do? It's very important as God's quarterback that you listen to what I am about to tell you. You need to hold onto this nugget for the rest of your life, because

I believe that where you are going you are going to need it. When you are operating out of the Power Formation, the Holy Spirit is going to tell you things that might blow your mind or cause you to wonder, "Where did that come from?" Don't be afraid. Trust the Holy Spirit. Why should you trust the Holy Spirit? The Lord told the disciples upon His departure that, "If you love me, you will keep my commandments. And I will ask the Father, and he will give you another Helper, to be with you forever, even the Spirit of truth, whom the world cannot receive, because it neither sees him nor knows him. You know him, for he dwells with you and will be in you" (**John 14:15-17**). Wow, there's a lot going on there but I want you to focus first and foremost on the fact that Holy Spirit is our Helper! The Holy Spirit was given to us to help us, not hinder us.

When we moved to Dallas so I could attend seminary upon the Holy Spirit's leading, it was one of the most exciting and also the most trying times of our lives as a young family. We went through a lot during that time and learned a lot. I would say the seminary experience caused us to lean on God like never before. I recall on one occasion my wife called me at work to tell me our car note was due and we only had $10 in our bank account. As God's quarterback, what do you do in that situation? My wife was looking for answers and I had nothing. I didn't know what to do. Then I heard the Holy Spirit say "Pray." That's what we did; my wife and I prayed on the phone and then I hung up and went back to work.

The next day at work my wife called me again. I noticed a different tone on the other end, when she said, "You will never guess what happened!"

I said, "Tell me."

She said, "Well, I was upstairs and the doorbell rang. It was FedEx and they had an envelope for us, and inside that envelope, there was a check for $1,000." We were floored but at that same time we both knew it was God who had answered our prayers. Here's the nugget in simplicity:

Where God guides, God provides!

Our Father has sent us the Holy Spirit to help us. In the verse mentioned above (**John 14:15-17**), the Holy Spirit lives in and dwells in us; that is why when you are in the Power Formation you will hear from God and He will provide direction. The other important part of that verse is the promise that the Holy Spirit will be with you forever. It is very comforting to know that in good times and in bad times the Holy Spirit won't abandon you. Sometimes you can feel abandoned but please know that you are not. The world may not understand or see the Holy Spirit, but you as a believer have the promise of God to know that the Holy Spirit is closer than you and I could ever imagine.

There is power in the Holy Spirit and when you receive that power, watch out, you can do amazing things. When you receive that power, you can do great things for the kingdom. As God's quarterback you have been called to do great things for the Lord. You will do things that you thought you could never do. You will conquer giants that you thought you could never defeat and climb heights you thought were beyond reach. I want to remind you though; it is not by your own power but by the power of the Holy Spirit. In the *Book of Acts*, the apostle Paul gives the account of Jesus talking to his disciples after He had come back. Jesus explains to them what will happen when the Holy Spirit comes. **Acts 1:8** is a powerful verse; Jesus says, "But you will receive power when the Holy Spirit comes on you." Power is one thing but the most important thing is what you to do with that power. The next part of that verse is life changing: "… and you will be my witnesses in Jerusalem, and in all Judea and Samaria, and to the ends of the earth." There is a purpose to the power.

The Baltimore Ravens bought into playing power football in a power formation for the sake of doing great things as a team. They realized that they may not garner the individual stats that other players on other teams are compiling, but that it's not about one individual person; it's about the whole team. The purpose of their offensive transformation was not about Lamar Jackson winning the MVP, nor was it for the sake of John Harbaugh winning

Coach of the Year. The purpose of the transformation to the Power Formation based offense was to take advantage of the skill set of the Baltimore Ravens' players for the sake of winning a Super Bowl.

The purpose of the Power Formation as God's quarterback is not for us to get glory for the things being done in our lives; it is for the sake of God's Kingdom. It's about building and strengthening God's kingdom. This book is not about me, nor is it about my love for football. This book is about helping build God's Kingdom. What is God asking you to do? What has God told you in private? Regardless of what it is, I urge you to get in alignment with God and get in the Power Formation of the Holy Trinity. Once you do, you are bound for success and I decree and declare it will be done. Just believe. Now get to work!

CHAPTER 6

The Passion

How do you define passion? I mean what does passion look like? If you saw passion walking down the street would you be able to recognize it? What are you passionate about? What are you drawn to? What grabs your attention? What can you absolutely not go without?

Passion is an interesting subject. Either you are passionate about something or you aren't. You cannot fake passion. When I look up the word *passion* in the dictionary, the definition reads: "something you are strongly interested in and enjoy." When you have passion, you have a strong interest. When you have passion, you have emotion; you are moved by whatever it is that you are passionate about.

For many years, I was searching round and round about what I was passionate about. During a time in my life not long ago, I was waffling about what my purpose was and asking myself, what did the good Lord put me on this earth to do? What was I called to do? What impact was I supposed to have on this world? How would I influence others? My wife asked me the simple question, "What are you passionate about?" Quite frankly, it was one of the hardest questions to answer. I just didn't know, and let me tell you, that was very frustrating. I mean I prayed. I fasted and felt like I wasn't getting any answers. I was stuck.

For years, I wanted to write a book but I'd start one and then stop. But this book was different. It finally hit me one day in church while we were living in Canada on an ex-pat assignment. God put in my spirit to write about something I was passionate about, with a twist. You see, as I mentioned before, I am a sports junkie, but I struggled with how that translated into being my passion. Let me tell you the amazing thing about our God; He makes the difficult things in our eyes simple. God told me, "Why don't you take the thing you are passionate about (sports) and use it for my glory to help build my kingdom?" So that's what I've done. This book is about my passion for sports intertwined with God's passion (more on this later) for us. He wants me to help His children by encouraging them to be His quarterback. So again I ask you:

What are *you* passionate about?

In the game of football, there are quarterbacks and then there are great quarterbacks. The great quarterbacks not only possess talent, but I would venture to say that they also possess, you guessed it, *passion*. The great ones love the game. They can't get enough of the game. They don't play for the money; they don't play for the accolades; and they don't play because someone is forcing them to. They play because they can't live without playing football. You hear some analysts and announcers say, "It's just in his blood." They were born to play quarterback. There's nothing like watching and playing with a quarterback that has passion about the game.

One quarterback I admire that played with great passion was Brett Favre. Now before I go any further about Brett Favre, I must admit that I didn't necessarily like him when he and the Green Bay Packers dismantled the New England Patriots in Super Bowl XXXI by the score of 35-21. Brett was the son of a football coach. Brett's dad coached him in high school and coached him hard. Brett Favre was about as passionate as they come. I mean he was a fiery son of a gun. He loved to play football and he played for a long time at a very high level. Favre was a Super Bowl champion and he won the MVP award. He played hurt and he played hard. He could be seen jawing at the other team. He was a quarterback who didn't back down from any opponent or challenge. Brett was full of passion. I'm reminded of the clip of him running down the field with his helmet off after he had thrown a touchdown pass to Andre Rison. Brett Favre looked like a little kid who had just thrown a pass in the backyard for the winning touchdown. Simply put, he loved the game.

In the college football ranks, probably the most passionate quarterback I remember during my lifetime has to be Tim Tebow, who played for the Florida Gators. Tim Tebow is probably also the most prolific quarterback in collegiate history. Tebow was an outstanding college quarterback, but more importantly, he's also a great person off the field. He is about one of the greatest examples of a person who lives for the Lord. He was a Heisman trophy winner his Sophomore year, a feat that had never been done prior by a Sophomore. He was also a first-team, college All-American twice. He led the Gators to a National Championship in 2009. Tim Tebow had a great college career and was a true leader of men.

What set Tim Tebow apart from the others? You guessed it, his passion. Tim Tebow had passion and his teammates followed him into battle every Saturday. I recall in a press conference after a loss to Ole Miss, Tebow said to the Florida Gator fans: "I promise you one thing, a lot of good will come out of this. You will never see any player in the entire country play as hard as I will play the rest of the season, and you will never see someone push the rest of the team as hard as I will push everybody the rest of the season, and you will never see a team play harder than we will the rest of the season. God bless." At the time, the Gators were 3-1. After that speech, Tebow led his team to 10 straight victories and a National Championship, defeating the Oklahoma Sooners 24-14. Tim Tebow had passion and he played and led with that same passion.

As God's quarterback we are in a position of great influence. There are chances on a daily basis to make a meaningful impact on people's lives that we come into contact with. We have been tasked with the responsibility of leading people in the game of life, and life as you know it can be hard. Would you want to follow someone who lacked passion or someone who exuded passion? Basically, what it boils down to is: do you care? Do you care about the people around you? Do you care about the people even when they don't care about you? Do you care about people even when you have been wronged?

> **As God's quarterback you have to care about God's people, or more profoundly, you have to <u>love</u> God's people.**

My youngest daughter, Cierra, reminds me a lot of myself. She is a sports junkie 2.0, a chip off the old block. We could be outside throwing the football one moment, kicking the soccer ball, and throwing the baseball around in the span of fifteen minutes. She can't get enough of sports. She will sit down and watch an entire ball game while emulating the moves of the players. She knows the teams and she knows their records and stats. She is passionate about sports. Again, she reminds me a lot of myself. Did I mention she is only nine years old? I'm excited to see how God will use her passion for sports as well.

Cierra has a pretty good memory, and as a matter of fact, for school she has to memorize Bible verses on a regular basis. Well, one of the verses she studied has to deal with how we treat each other, how we should be passionate about one another. The verse talks about how we need to "love" not only the people who treat us well, but how we also must "love" our enemies too. In **Matthew 5:43-48**, Jesus says, "You have heard that it was said, 'You shall love your neighbor and hate your enemy.' But I say to you, Love your enemies and pray for those who persecute you, so that you may be sons of your Father who is in heaven. For He makes his sun rise on the evil and on the good, and sends rain on the just and on the unjust. For if you love those who love you, what reward do you have? Do not even the tax collectors do the same? And if you greet only your brothers, what more are you doing than others? Do not even the Gentiles do the same? You therefore must be perfect, as your heavenly Father is perfect." Being passionate about God's people can be messy business and sometimes it can be painful, but we are called as God's quarterbacks to love all His people.

When I think about passion, I'd be remiss not to say who God's most passionate quarterback was; that would be none other than God's only begotten son, Jesus Christ. Without any doubt, Jesus Christ epitomizes passion. In 2004, the much anticipated movie about Jesus came out titled *The Passion of the Christ*, and it did not disappoint. The movie was a very vivid depiction of Jesus's passion for mankind. He was beaten; He was ostracized; He was hung on a cross at Golgotha. He bore our sins on that cross so we could have life eternal. His selfless and sacrificial act would save the world from their sins. His passion wasn't just for those who believed; during that time He died for those who didn't believe, who would one day believe. The same people that were crucifying him He was dying for. On the cross, He would go on to say, "Father, forgive them, for they know not what they do" (**Luke 23:34**).

I remember watching that movie and hearing sniffles and seeing tears of those in the theater as Jesus was being flogged with an apparatus that tore at his flesh as he writhed in pain. I remember thinking to myself that no one else would endure such a sacrifice for me, or you for that matter. Jesus's passion is unmatched. His love for us runs so deep that it ought to let us know how special we are in his eyes. He cares so much for you and I that He gave up His life for us. As God's quarterback, we are called to be selfless in our dealings with others. It's all about serving others.

In **Mark 10:45**, Jesus says, "For the Son of Man did not come to be served but to serve and give his life as a ransom for many." I'm reminded of how quarterbacks at times have to stand in the pocket and hold onto the ball a little bit longer and take a crushing hit in order to deliver the ball to the wide receiver. The quarterback sacrifices himself for the sake of the team. In the same way, we as God's quarterbacks have to sacrifice ourselves for God's people. We have to remember as we are serving that it is not about us—remember there is no "I" in "team." As Jesus did, be of service to others with passion.

4TH QUARTER

"

The pursuit of greatness takes courage. The pursuit of greatness takes hard work. The pursuit of greatness takes confidence.

CHAPTER 7

The Prize

As long as I can remember, I've always been competitive. It doesn't matter if we are playing *Monopoly* or *Tic-Tac-Toe*; I play to win. Yes, I am that dad who gets a little too amped up at my kid's soccer game or baseball game, but as I said before, I play to win. Now with that being said, I play fair and by the rules. Let me also add if I lose (I don't like losing), I believe in good sportsmanship. Matter of fact, that is one thing that I have taught my son, Trey (Ross III), about losing: be a good sport. My son is a smart kid. He pays attention and I've noticed that he has taken this lesson to heart.

You see, my son and I work out together in the mornings, usually around 6:00 a.m. (sometimes earlier). For our cardio workout, we usually either run on the treadmill or play one-on-one basketball. The hoops games can get pretty competitive. Sometimes he wins, sometimes I win. Either way we always shake hands and say, "Good game."

My son has learned that good sportsmanship is important. But guess what? He plays to win even if it means beating his old man. As God's quarterback we play to win!

I remember playing football as a kid in high school. The season started in August, the hottest days of the year. Before we put on a helmet or shoulder pads we had to get into shape. I can recall despising this time of the season because we would run until we could run no more. In some instances, guys would be doubled over puking up their breakfast or lunch, while the coach barked, "On the line, let's go. Again." Sprints were the worst. I said breakfast or lunch because we would have doubles or triples; in other words, two or three practices a day. It was during those days I believe the coach was separating the men from the boys. I think he wanted to see who really wanted to be a part of his team. Not one time during those brutal practices or weightlifting sessions or rehab sessions was I thinking about coming in second place. We weren't doing this for a silver medal or a consolation prize. We were practicing to win; we were hurting to win; we were lifting to win. It was about winning the prize and that prize for our high school football team was the state title. Now, before you go on wondering if we ever won the state title, the quick answer is "No," but that was the goal. That was what drove us to train hard and perform at our absolute best.

Now, if someone tells you that winning isn't everything, I wouldn't say they are completely wrong; but I would say winning should be the goal. In the game of professional football, the prize is winning the Super Bowl and earning the Lombardi trophy. There's something moving about watching a grown man hold up that trophy and sob with great joy over something he has been chasing since the day he molded his first mouthpiece. It's a pretty awesome sight. After all those training camps, playing in unfathomable conditions and in great pain, they finally reach the pinnacle. Some guys never get to the Super Bowl and some do but never win. I'm reminded of Jim Kelly, the former quarterback of the Buffalo Bills who had made it to four Super Bowls. That's right, four and Kelly's team lost every single one. Losing four Super Bowls is a daunting thing, but I know one thing is for sure, Jim Kelly never once decided to give up the pursuit of the prize. Jim Kelly is a fighter in more ways than one (keep fighting, Jim!).

In the game of life as God's quarterback, we have a goal. There is a prize that we are after, something more valuable than a trophy. The goal I speak of is to save souls, or I should say, introduce lost souls to our Lord and Savior, Jesus Christ. That is the ultimate prize. God has called you to a great work, a life-altering work with eternal consequences. There's nothing more exciting than sharing the gospel with someone and seeing them accept Jesus Christ into their life. We could obtain accolades, money, and fame, but all of those are temporary and we can't take them with us. But to have your name written in the Lamb's book of life is permanent. I challenge you to be aware of your environment and who you come into contact with. Is there someone in your circle who needs an invitation to accept Jesus Christ?

I shared earlier on what Jesus Christ did on that cross at Golgotha. He hung on that cross and died a death that we should have died in order for us to live a life that resembles His. In the gospel of Matthew in the 28th chapter, Jesus commands the disciples and us to partake in the "Great Commission" when he says in verse 19, "All authority in heaven and on earth has been given to me. Go therefore and make disciples of all nations, baptizing them in the name of the Father and of the Son and of the Holy Spirit, teaching them to observe all that I have commanded you. And behold I am with you always, to the end of the age." Wow, what a message! Jesus is not just asking us; he's telling us, demanding us to carry out this important task. Here's the thing, Jesus is not telling us to do this by ourselves. He will be with us every step of the way. He's calling you to greatness and He's calling you to disciple other quarterbacks for His heavenly Father. Here's the question: will you help Him build the kingdom? Will you strive for the prize?

As I reach the half-way point of this chapter, the NFL playoffs are upon us and there are some amazing quarterbacks leaving it on the field. I am in football heaven (excuse the metaphor), but I really am because it's also the week of the College Football Playoff Championship with unbeaten Clemson playing against unbeaten LSU—what a matchup! I might add there are two talented quarterbacks playing, but I want to talk about a former Clemson alum by the name of Deshaun Watson. Deshaun Watson is a quarterback that is destined for greatness; he's just a flat-out winner. He's cool under pressure and really knows how to rally his troops in the face of adversity. He's won a National Championship on the collegiate level by way of a 4th-quarter comeback in the waning moments against the heralded Alabama Crimson Tide. I believe one day he will win a Super Bowl; it's just a matter of time.

So why do I bring up Deshaun Watson while talking about saving souls for Christ? Let me explain. During the biggest moments of his football career, he doesn't shy away from greatness. Some folks are afraid of greatness, why is that? Here's why:

The pursuit of greatness takes courage.

The pursuit of greatness takes hard work.

The pursuit of greatness takes confidence.

You have to have a certain righteous swagger, if you know what I mean. You have to know that, "no weapon formed against you will prosper" (**Isaiah 54:17**), and "that if God be for us who can be against us" (**Romans 8:31**).

In the AFC Wild Card game of the Houston Texans against the Buffalo Bills, Deshaun Watson made an incredible play; while being attacked on both sides, he spun away from the would-be defenders and threw a perfect pass to his running back out in the flat, who proceeded to run for a first down. After the game was over, when reporters asked Deshaun how he pulled off that play, he said, "Someone had to be great today, why not me?"

Here's what I ask of you today: are you chasing greatness? Are you chasing the prize? Are you willing to go out there when life is on the line—not the game—but when *life* is on the line and make *disciples*. I urge you to take action now and go do it; there's nothing more exhilarating.

The funny thing about winning the prize on the football field and off the field is there are a lot of parallels. They both require sacrifice; they both require giving up your body. The pursuit of the prize requires you to give up your time, and most of all, it requires you to get out of your comfort zone. The main difference between winning the Vince Lombardi trophy and winning souls for Christ is everybody can win souls, only a few can win the Lombardi. There are souls waiting to be saved. When Jesus looked out to the crowds he saw the multitudes. He had compassion for them, and he said to the disciples, "The harvest is plentiful, but the laborers are few; therefore pray earnestly to the Lord of the harvest to send out laborers into his harvest" (**Matthew 9:37-38**).

God is looking for quarterbacks to get on the field and win the prize (lost souls).

CHAPTER 8

The Press Conference

Historically, the quarterback has been considered the face of the franchise. He is usually the most recognizable player on the field. In the stands, kids and adults don the jerseys of their favorite quarterback. The top-selling jerseys are often replicas of the best quarterbacks in the league. The quarterback tends to be the center of attention. In football-speak, you live or die by the play of your quarterback. The QB can be the reason for the team's success or their failure. When you are building a football roster, the most important position that you must solidify first and foremost is, you guessed it, the quarterback.

In the history of the NFL draft, a quarterback has been drafted with the first pick more than any other position. They are highly scouted, highly touted, and highly watched. What's more important is not only how they carry themselves on the field but also how they carry themselves off the field. I've titled this chapter "The Press Conference" because I want to focus on how the quarterback represents the franchise with his words, actions, and demeanor. It's during the press conference that you get to see the character and makeup of the quarterback. As God's quarterback how will you represent the Creator of the Universe? As God's quarterback how will you handle the spotlight? As God's quarterback how will you deal with those who criticize you and critique you? Will you lead with poise and humility? Will you let your light shine? Will you give Him glory?

The Philadelphia Eagles won Super Bowl LII against the New England Patriots led by their backup quarterback, Nick Foles. Foles also pulled off one of the most successful trick plays in Super Bowl history, known as the "Philly Special." It was a play where Foles handed the ball to a running back who then pitched to the tight end who was running in the opposite direction. Meanwhile, Foles snuck into the end zone and caught a pass from the tight end. It was a great trick play. Check it out for yourselves because my play by play does it no justice. With that being said, it's not the quarterback's play that I want to highlight, but his character and his witness. Nick Foles was later traded to the Jacksonville Jaguars, and in the first game of the season, he broke his clavicle. After hearing that you have to imagine that Foles was devastated and frustrated; but if you think that, then you don't know Nick Foles. In a press conference, a reporter asked him did he ever have doubt after getting injured and losing his starting position. Without hesitation, he told the reporter that his faith in God is greater than the game of football. He went on to say that it's not about him, it's not about us, and that his purpose is greater than football. He shared that his ministry is the men in that locker room and ministering to them. Nick Foles's purpose is representing the Lord Jesus Christ, hurt or not hurt, at all times. The Bible tells us in **Colossians 3:17**: "And whatever you do, in word or deed, do everything in the name of the Lord Jesus, giving thanks to God the Father through Him."

We have to understand that God is bigger than our problems, that God is bigger than our setbacks. God is bigger than our failures. He's greater than a job that we got let go from because the company wanted to go in a different direction. Similar to what Nick Foles was saying, our faith ought not be in the material things or our occupations; but our faith needs to be in God and that's the message we need to preach. We must understand that tough times in life will come, and I believe God tests us to see how we will respond. What will your post game press conference look like? Remember these two verses: "And we know that in all things God works for the good of those who love him, who have been called according to his purpose" (**Romans 8:28**). Everything is working for your good, hold onto that. The other verse you need to store away in your mind is **Psalm 30:5**: "Weeping may endure for a night, but joy cometh in the morning." When you are going through hard times, don't forget that "this too shall pass." Your trouble is temporary. Keep the faith and continue to fight through adversity as God's quarterback.

After I had announced my call to ministry over twenty years ago, I remember a meeting that my senior pastor called with the deacon and the deaconess board to further announce my call. It was a very exciting time for me and a very emotional time as well, for I knew my life would never be the same. It was during that meeting I learned a valuable lesson that I will never forget. At the time, it didn't make sense but I fully understood the lesson as time progressed. Inside the meeting room, all the deacons and deaconesses were sitting around the large oval table with me at the head of the table. Each person in attendance went around the room and congratulated me with words of encouragement and wisdom. They wished me the best and I was very appreciative of their support. There was one deacon, however, who had something different to say, and his name was Deacon Willie Jackson. Deacon Jackson was a man of small stature but his faith and courage was immense. I remember like it was yesterday; he looked me in my eye and said, "Son, I want you to remember one thing: you ain't no better than anybody else." I was shocked at what I heard. Why would he rain on my parade? It just didn't seem encouraging, and now that I look back on it, it wasn't supposed to be. I definitely took it the wrong way then, but what I heard years later was "Stay humble. It's not about you." Deacon Jackson was simply trying to keep me grounded.

As God's quarterback, the Lord wants us to carry ourselves with humility. No matter the accolades we obtain or a certain status that we reach, he wants us to remain humble. But even more important, the Lord wants to receive the glory. You see, as God's quarterback, we have what this world needs and that's Jesus. We are his hands and feet. We are a reflection of Him and are from Him, therefore we have influence and we can bring understanding to those who are lost. When Jesus delivered the Sermon on the Mount, he told his followers, "You are the salt of the earth…you are the light of the world. A city set on a hill cannot be hidden. Nor do people light a lamp and put it under a basket, but on a stand, and it gives light to all in the house. In the same way let your light shine before others, so that they may see your good works and give glory to your Father who is heaven" (**Matthew 5:13-16**). We have a responsibility to be the salt and light. God has given us all unique gifts and talents and He has called us to do good works for kingdom purposes. More importantly, He wants to receive the glory when we carry out the good works that He enables us to do.

My oldest daughter, Briyana, is a gifted dancer and singer. She has performed in numerous settings and venues. As of late, she has even written several songs and created the music as well to accompany those lyrics. It's funny because she is a shy young lady, but when the lights come on and the music plays, she becomes a different person. She's a performer and loves performing. She's had people come up to her after competitions, plays, and recitals and tell her how they were moved by her performance. We try to make sure she understands that she is representing her heavenly Father when she performs and that He deserves all the glory. There's nothing I love more than to see someone publicly giving God the glory for something they were able to accomplish. That's all He wants is the glory. As God's quarterback, are you going to use your gifts and talents in order that He may get the glory?

POST-GAME ANALYSIS

"

You must do something with the talent that God gave you.

CHAPTER 9

Time of Possession

As I write this chapter from the backseat of an Uber on the way to the Toronto Pearson Airport, the thing that I have noticed as I get older is that time is precious. I wish I had more of it this morning when the 5:30a.m. wake-up call rang my phone. Time seems to go by faster and faster as I get older. The days seem to fly by. One day it's Monday; I blink and it's Friday. When I look at my kids, they are no longer babies. My oldest, for Pete's sake, has a mustache and eats more than his father. By the way, he has the physique of a Mr. Olympia.

I sometimes wonder, however, where did the time go so fast? One thing is for sure, Father Time has been kind to my wife; she hasn't aged a bit. She still has her girlish figure and recently someone asked me if she was my daughter (she loved that compliment, by the way). My wife still melts my butter. What an amazing woman, wife, and mother. I'm thankful to God for my wife and kids and the memories He has allowed us to make together. Each day is a blessing and a precious gift from God. Time is a precious commodity that is invaluable, and as God's quarterback, you must make the most of it.

I've titled this chapter "Time of Possession" because in the game of football usually the team that controls the "Time of Possession" has a better chance of winning the game. Time of Possession is the amount of time that the offense has control of the football. On the flipside, it's the time the opposing defense has been on the field. As I mentioned before, time is precious in the game of life but on the football field as well. The longer the offense can stay on the field, the better chance they have at winning the game, because they are able to wear the defense down and impose their will. In the playoffs especially, every possession of the ball is extremely important, and what you do with each possession is of equal importance. The stakes are raised in the playoffs because there is more on the line. Again, everyone is striving for the prize, the Lombardi trophy. The playoffs are where legends are made, and during the 2020 NFC Championship game, Aaron Rodgers and the Green Bay Packers squared off against the San Francisco 49ers to determine who would represent the NFC in the Super Bowl. Leading up to the game, Aaron expressed that he thinks about getting to and winning a second Super Bowl every day. Winning a second Super Bowl would put him in the upper echelon of quarterbacks in NFL history. He knows, however, that as he gets older that he won't have as many opportunities to be a Super Bowl champion once again. His sense of urgency is heightened, and we too need to have that same sense of urgency to do what God has called upon us to do (by the way, Aaron, I hope you get there).

What are you putting off doing today that you think you can wait for tomorrow? What has God called you to do that you are procrastinating? Has God called you to write a book, go back to school, start your own business or ministry? What is it that you know you must do but are delaying for whatever reason? Maybe someone has discouraged you in the past or you failed at a previous attempt and are afraid to try again. Maybe you don't think you are worthy or qualified to do what it is God has laid on your heart. If God has given you a dream or an assignment then you are qualified. Here's the thing: you can do it but not on your own.

You need God to fulfill your mission.

In the Gospel according to John, Jesus tells us the following, "Abide in me, and I in you. As the branch cannot bear fruit by itself, unless it abides in the vine, neither can you, unless you abide in me. I am the vine; you are the branches. Whoever abides in me and I in him, it is he that bears much fruit, for apart from me you can do nothing" (**John 15:4-5**).

We can't do anything when we rely on our own strength, but we can do all things through Christ. He is our source of strength but we must tap into Him. Perhaps God has been tugging at your heart to join His family but you are delaying. Don't wait. Take a step of faith and have your life changed forever. I promise you that you will have no regrets. For those quarterbacks who are already on God's team I want to challenge you. Sometimes we can get a little complacent in following our purpose. I say "we" because I'm speaking to myself as well. If we are not careful, we can lose the gift and talents that God has given us if we don't use them. In the parable of the talents in the Gospel according to Matthew, three servants are given three different monetary values (talents) from their master. One servant takes his five talents and trades them, resulting in five additional talents. The second servant takes his two talents and likewise doubles his talents to equal four talents. The last servant receives one talent and buries it, doing nothing.

Don't bury your talent, don't waste it. Put your talent to good use serving your God-given purpose.

When the master returns he tells the first two, "Well done, good and faithful servant. You have been faithful over a little; I will set you over much. Enter into in the joy of the Master" (**Matthew 25:23**). Now the last servant doesn't quite get the resounding affirmation, instead this is what is said to him because he hid his talent, "You wicked and slothful servant…So take the talent from him and give it to him who has ten talents" (**Matthew 25:26,28**). Seems harsh but God is expecting a return on his investment.

You may receive more or less talent than your quarterback colleagues, but the point of emphasis is:

You must do something with the talent that God gave you.

The key to remember is that it's not what you have, it's what you do with what you have. In the beginning of this book, I stated that God's quarterbacks come in all different shapes and sizes. They also come with different gifts and talents. Don't compare yourself to other quarterbacks; just be the best quarterback you can be for God, using your unique set of skills, talents, and passion. Your situation may not be the same as your counterpart, but that doesn't prohibit you from carrying out your assignment. In essence, if you are slack in using your gifts or talents, you can go from a starting quarterback to sitting on the bench. God can use whomever He wants to use for His purposes, and if you are not willing to be used by Him, He moves onto the next individual ready to step up. Sounds harsh but there is work to be done for the kingdom.

In the book of Ecclesiastes, especially in Chapter 3, the word of God references that there is a time for everything. "For everything, there is a season" (**Ecclesiastes 3:1**). I mentioned Aaron Rodgers and his quest for a second Super Bowl trophy and how he was cognizant of the fact that he didn't have too many chances to do it. Well, there was a time when Aaron Rodgers was a backup quarterback with the Green Bay Packers, not because he was wasting his talent, but because it just wasn't his time yet to be elevated to a starting quarterback. Aaron Rodgers, a future Hall of Famer, was sitting behind Brett Favre, now a Hall of Famer. Aaron prepared himself though and he was more than ready when his time came. Now, as God's quarterback, you may be in a situation where you haven't received your assignment, but I encourage you as you wait in the wings to prepare yourself by reading God's word and praying for clarity, or better yet, for your purpose. When you get your chance, will you be ready?

Before I wrap up this book, I want to say thank you for being open to receive what God has laid on my heart to share with you. He has taken my love for football and my love for Him and commingled the two to create a book, and more importantly, a resource to encourage and enlist existing and future quarterbacks to the playing field. My hope is that there is something that spoke to you within these pages that will make an impact on you as you strive to live for Him and obtain the prize of the high calling. If you have made a decision to follow Christ during the reading of this book, I want to be the first to say, "Welcome to the family." Last but not least, I want to speak a blessing over your life as you move forward as God's quarterback.

Special Blessing:

I decree and declare that this will be the year you take hold of what God has birthed in you and bring it to fruition. I decree and declare that this year you will have a monumental impact for the kingdom. You will fight through your fears and procrastination. I decree and declare that you will walk with purpose and with the power of the Holy Spirit. I decree and declare that you will live for the Lord and give Him the glory in all that you do!

Now, go and be the quarterback that God wants you to be and become!!!

THE GAME PLAN

9 Scripted Plays for God's Quarterback

1. Join God's team and become His quarterback by confessing to Jesus Christ that you are ready.
2. Read God's playbook (the Bible).
3. Step into your leadership role. You are God's quarterback.
4. Be alert. Satan and his team are on the attack.
5. Use your unique gifts and talents for the kingdom.
6. Remember why you are doing this—because of your compassion for others.
7. Win souls and make disciples.
8. Give God the glory in all that you do.
9. Time is precious. Make the most of it.

SCRIPTURE INDEX

Chapter 1 –The Pardon

Romans 10:9

Chapter 2 – The Playbook

Romans 8:38-39

2 Timothy 2:15

Chapter 3 – The Position

James 1:22

Philippians 4:13

Chapter 4 – The Pass Rush

1 Peter 5:8

James 4:7

Psalm 46:10

Chapter 5 – The Power Formation

Philippians 1:6

John 14:15-17

Acts 1:8

Chapter 6 – The Passion

Matthew 5:43-48

Luke 23:34

Mark 10:45

Chapter 7 – The Prize

Matthew 28:19

Isaiah 54:17

Romans 8:31

Matthew 9:37-38

Chapter 8 – The Press Conference

Colossians 3:17

Romans 8:28

Psalm 30:5

Matthew 5:13-16

Chapter 9 – Time of Possession

John 15:4-5

Matthew 25:23

Matthew 25:26,28

Ecclesiastes 3:1

ABOUT THE AUTHOR

Ross E. Wyche Jr. is an avid sports fan who has spent his professional career in the entertainment industry, oil & gas sector, and full-time ministry. An entrepreneur, he got his start selling penny candy to his classmates in elementary school. He has counseled and advised people from all walks of life: professional athletes, clergy, married couples, and countless people needing encouragement. Some would say Ross has never met a stranger.

He completed his BS in Accounting from the University of Massachusetts and his MBA with a concentration in Finance from Morgan State University. He also earned a ThM (Masters of Theology degree) with a concentration in pastoral ministry from Dallas Theological Seminary. He is happily married to his wife and best friend, Niya. They have a son, Ross III, and two daughters, Briyana and Cierra. In his spare time, Ross enjoys reading, watching sports, and road trips with his family.

Manufactured by Amazon.ca
Bolton, ON